THE Reivers

by

JOHN GRANT

1981

JAMES THIN
The Mercat P
Edinburgh

First published in Great Britain in 1981

Enquiries should be sent to the publisher at the undernoted address:

JAMES THIN
The Mercat Press, 55 South Bridge
Edinburgh, Scotland

ISBN 0 901824 66 6

Printed in Great Britain by:

Alna Press Ltd, Broxburn, Scotland

AND... this is how it all began*...

Once upon a time there was an Island, and it was divided into two Kingdoms. The Kingdom at the top was called Scotland, and the lower down one was called England.

The people who lived at the ends or around the edges of the Island were fairly confident of their place in the scheme of things.... but, in the middle it was all somewhat confused!

Not that this seems to have worried the Scots... not even James, their King.

As Kings go, James was somewhat different! He was much given to dressing up and wandering about in a pretty informal manner, getting himself involved in fights and other un-King-like adventures.

CRAMOND BRIG

But.... James had an Uncle Henry, who was anything <u>but</u> informal.

Uncle Henry was King of England..... and he never did anything that was not carefully planned. He liked everything and everybody to be just <u>so</u>.... even his Queen, and anyone who wasn't.. well, that's another and altogether unpleasant story.

When King Henry wanted to tour his realm <u>he</u> didn't go wandering off by himself. He worked everything out down to the smallest detail.

And <u>that</u> included the route.

However..........

* .. on the other hand it may be just a made-up story.

FROM THAT DAY ON . . . . .

EXCUSE ME, SIR. IS THIS **SCOTLAND** OR **ENGLAND** ?

A DEBATABLE POINT, SIR, INDEED !

NO **KING** !

NO **LAW** !

UTOPIA !

. . . IT WAS CALLED THE **DEBATABLE LAND** . . .

AS **MARCH WARDEN** I ARREST YOU IN THE NAME OF THE **KING** !

GO AND ARREST YOUR **GRANNY** . . . . THIS IS THE **DEBATABLE LAND** !

KILNOCKIE WELCOMES CAREFUL RIDERS

2a

BLACK DICK SIMSON, NINTH LAIRD OF KILNOCKIE, SITS DOWN TO DINE . . . . . .

WHERE'S MY **BEEF** WOMAN ?

WHAT'S THIS ?

NOT . . . THE **SPURS** !

YES !

THE **SPURS** !!

LADY GRIZEL, CHATELAINE OF THE TOWER OF KILNOCKIE, HAS MADE THE **ULTIMATE GESTURE** OF THE REIVER'S WIFE . . . . THE LARDER IS EMPTY . . . . TIME TO **GET REIVING** !

THE **SIMSONS** OF KILNOCKIE RIDE OUT TO PRACTISE THE ANCIENT TRADE OF THE **BORDER REIVER***

* Reiver, n. a robber, a freebooter.

Chambers Scots Dictionary.

2b

A-REIVING ♫ A-REIVING— SINCE REIVING'S **BIN** MY RUE-AYE-IN...

THE SIMSONS RIDE OUT........

HI, CAPTAIN.... WHERE'RE WE **GOING**?

TO PAY A VISIT ON THE **KERRS***....

I HAPPEN TO KNOW THAT **THEY** ARE OFF RAIDING THE ELIOTS

* HISTORICAL NOTE:- ...**NOT** THE TERRIBLE KERRS OF CESSFORD.. ...**NOR** THE WILD KERRS OF FERNIEHIRST..... BUT THE **KERRS OF SCUNNERDUBS**·A CLAN OF REIVERS ONLY EQUALLED FOR SHEER INCOMPETENCE BY THE SIMSONS OF KILNOCKIE.

THERE IT IS, LADS. **SCUNNERDUBS** TOWER... ...AND NOT A KERR IN SIGHT!

AWAY YOU GO, SHUGGIE.....MAKE SURE THERE ARE **NO MEN**!

THREE CRAWS (SAT UPON A WA')

MEN? MEN? MEN? MEN? MEN? MEN? ?

3a

NO **MEN**, CAPTAIN!

...AND **NO CATTLE** EITHER!

THE CUNNING DEVILS...NEVER TRUST A KERR...!

THE FIRST CRAW FELL AND BROKE ITS JAW!

THEY'LL'VE HIDDEN THEM... ...IN THE **BOGLE'S BROSE-POT**!

FORWARD, LADS! WE'LL SOON HAVE THE HERD OUT OF THE BROSE-POT... ..AND??

CAPTAIN, WE WILL FOLLOW YOU TO THE **ENDS OF THE EARTH**.... ..EVEN AS FAR AS **GLASGOW**.... ..BUT **NOT** INTO THE **BROSE POT**!!! HAVE YOU FORGOTTEN THE **BOGLE**????

THE DREADED **WHIGMALEERIE**!

3b

BY A WINDING TRACK KNOWN ONLY TO THE KERRS OF SCUNNERDUBS, THE SIMSONS OF KILNOCKIE, THE ARMSTRONGS, ELIOTS, MUSGRAVES, GRAEMES, NIXONS AND ONE OR TWO OTHERS....
....DEEPER AND DEEPER INTO THE SINISTER DEPTHS OF THE GORGE.....

16a

16b

SO — WHAT GIVES WITH ALL THE **RACKET**?

YOU WANT TO PAWN YOUR MORION OR YOUR ARQUEBUS — COME BACK IN THE MORNING.. SHOP'S **SHUT**!

I'M **MARTIN**!

SO! I SHOULD OPEN UP BECAUSE YOU'RE **MARTIN**? I'M SOLLY **ROSENBLOOM**. ...AND THE SHOP STAYS **SHUT**! CLEAR OFF OR I'LL CALL THE **WATCH**!!

BUT — I'M MARTIN FROM **KILNOCKIE**!

OUR FAMILIES USED TO DO BUSINESS — IN **CATTLE**!

THAT'S IT, THEN.... 6 COWS, 2 BULLS, 3 HEIFERS.. **N.Q.A.**

SIGN HERE..

N.Q.A. — NO QUESTIONS ASKED!

...AND IF ANYONE ASKS — THEY FELL OFF THE BACK OF A WAGON!

CATTLE?

OH...**THAT** MARTIN.. ..YOUR PEOPLE SUPPLIED US WITH CATTLE **WHOLESALE**. ..OR SOMETHING!

WHY DIDN'T YOU **SAY**? WAIT THERE..I'M **COMING DOWN**!

17a

COME IN, MARTIN... **MY OLD FRIEND**...THAT I SHOULD LEAVE YOU AND YOUR COMPANIONS OUTSIDE ALL NIGHT!

GOLDA! REBECCA! SET **SIX** EXTRA PLACES!

NO FATTED CALF?

WHAT IS IT THIS TIME? A SURPRISE BARMITZVAH?

UNCLE EFREM WILL HAVE AN **AUDIENCE** BEYOND HIS WILDEST DREAMS!

UNCLE EFREM? **AUDIENCE**?

GREAT — UNCLE, ON MY MOTHER'S SIDE. ..A NOTED **RABBI** AND A **GREAT POET**!

TROUBLE IS HE CAN'T GET PEOPLE TO LISTEN!

UNCLE, MEET MARTIN AND HIS FRIENDS..

MARTIN, MEET THE GREATEST POET OF THE AGE..... ...RABBI **BURNZ**!

17b

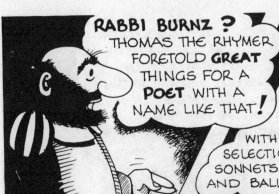

RABBI BURNZ? THOMAS THE RHYMER FORETOLD **GREAT** THINGS FOR A **POET** WITH A NAME LIKE THAT!

HM! VERY **PERCEPTIVE**, THOMAS OF ERCILDOUNE! WHEN SOLLY'S TABLE HAS FEASTED YOUR BODIES, I WILL **REFRESH** YOUR **SPIRITS** WITH A SELECTION OF SONNETS, ODES AND BALLADS!

Wee, modest, crimson-tippit beastie!

WHAT'S HE TALKING ABOUT?

HE'S A **POET**.... ..POETS TEND TO TALK **FUNNY**!

OH! A **POET**! HI, MR BURNZ, I KNOW A **POEM**... ...THERE WAS A YOUNG LADY FROM GRETNA.. .WHO TOOK OFF HER....

SHUGGIE

SORRY CAPTAIN! |18a|

A FINE REPAST INDEED, MR ROSENBLOOM, SIR. ESPECIALLY THE SOUP!

YES.. CHICKEN WITH **MATZO BALLS**.. ..REBECCA'S SPECIALITY

TELL ME SOMETHING MARTIN! WHAT IS IT SHUGGIE?

WHAT SORT OF A BEAST IS A **MATZO**?

.. AND NOW — THE MOMENT WE'VE ALL BEEN WAITING FOR... WITH READINGS FROM HIS LATEST MASTERPIECES ..RABBI BURNZ!

O, WAD SOME POW'R THE GIFTIE GIE US..... TAE SEE **SOME** FOLK BEFORE **THEY** SEE US!!

THE RABBI'S PERFORMANCE IS HEROIC.....BUT AFTER A LONG, ACTION-PACKED DAY, A MEAL, AND NOW A BLAZING FIRE.... ..ONE..BY ONE...THE....AUDIENCE.....NODS.....**OFF**. |18b|

NOT A LIGHT IS TO BE SEEN IN THE PRE-DAWN DARKNESS SHROUDING THE STREETS OF CARLISLE.

WATCHMAN! WHAT OF THE NIGHT?

WELL? WHAT OF IT?

YOU'RE RIGHT! IT IS A DAFT SORT OF QUESTION!

..BUT, NOT MANY MILES TO THE SOUTH, A LIGHT SHOWS HIGH IN THE GREAT FORTRESS OF NETHERBY... SEAT OF THE MIGHTY GRAEMES... AND BOWER OF THE FAIR ELLEN.

IT IS TIME, M'LADY!

EH? TIME? WHAT AM I WEARING TODAY?

WEARING? YOUR WEDDING GOWN, OF COURSE!

OH, GOD! I'D FORGOTTEN... I'M GETTING MARRIED...TO CYRIL OF SILLOTH...AND IT SHOULD HAVE BEEN... (SIGH!)...TO... YOUNG LOCHINVAR!

19a

WHAT DO YOU THINK, DEVORGILLA?

CYRIL?.... A RIGHT WEE NYAFF!

HOW DARE YOU!!

BONK!

A MERE SERVANT.. SPEAKING OF MY BETROTHED LIKE THAT!

SIGH!

BUT.... YOU'RE RIGHT!

TIME TO PREPARE YOURSELF, M'LADY.. ..DAWN IS NIGH!

YES..TODAY THE RITUAL MUST GIVE ME STRENGTH FOR THE ORDEAL TO COME..

IS ALL READY?

YES, M'LADY.... BELL, BOOK.. ..AND CANDLE!

19b

MEANWHILE... BACK AT THE **CARLISLE EQUITABLE LOAN CO.** EST. 1539

GOOD MORNING, GENTLEMEN. YOU SLEPT WELL, I TRUST. I MUST GO DOWN TO THE SHOP... THE WOMEN WILL GIVE YOU BREAKFAST.

THANKS, SOLLY. WE'LL DO THE SAME FOR YOU IF YOU'RE EVER IN KILNOCKIE!

MAGIC PORRIDGE, MRS REBECCA!

THANK YOU, SHUGGIE... I'VE PACKED SOME BLINTZES TO EAT ON YOUR WAY.

A **WORD**, SHUGGIE... I WISH YOU'D **STOP** RECITING THOSE AWFUL **POEMS**.. PARTICULARLY IN **COMPANY**..... "THERE WAS A YOUNG LADY OF GRETNA...." ..**INDEED!** WHAT MUST RABBI BURNZ HAVE **THOUGHT?**

OH, HE'D **HEARD** IT, CAPTAIN. HE TOLD ME A NEW POEM: "THERE WAS AN OLD MAN OF DUMFRIES, WHO HAD A BIG...."

SORRY, CAPTAIN!

21a

FINE DAY FOR A **WEDDING!**

DON'T **SAY** THINGS LIKE THAT!

HER MAJESTYS THEATRE — HAMLET — A NEW THRILLER BY W. SHAKSPEAR Three Nights

WHAT TIME **IS** THE WEDDING?

NOON!

NOON? IT'S AFTER ELEVEN NOW!

WE'LL BE **TOO LATE!**

IT'S **NEVER** TOO LATE FOR A HERD OF GRAEME COWS...

..AND.. OF COURSE THE HAND OF THE **FAIR ELLEN!**

WHAT'S THE **HOLD-UP** IN FRONT?

I'D FORGOTTEN... IT'S **MARKET DAY**... WE'LL BE AGES GETTING THROUGH ALL THIS LOT!!

I WILL ENJOY THEE NOW, MY CELIA, COME!

GET AWAY.. ..DIRTY OLD MAN....IN ANY CASE MY NAME'S AMARYLLIS!

I'M NOT ASKING 5 GROATS.. OR EVEN 4...

IT'S A DEAL, THEN, JACK! THE MAGIC BEANS FOR YOUR MOTHER'S COW.

IS IT TRUE WHAT THEY SAY ABOUT TOM-A-TOES?

...ACTUALLY, WE'VE SEEN 'HAMLET'..IN LONDON..AT THE GLOBE..BIT PSYCHOLOGICAL FOR MY TASTE!

POT-A-TOES! ..FRESH IN FROM THE NEW WORLD

I'M LOOKING FOR SOMETHING WHICH EXPLORES THE BASIC NATURE OF HUMAN RELATIONSHIP.

HABERS DASHED

CHAPMAN BILLY BOOKSELLER

YOU WANT DIRTY BOOKS?

COD PIECES? —NO, SIR— TRY THE HABERDASHER

HELLO, LITTLE SHODDY!

HELLO, BIGMOUTH!

21b

A **VERY** SATISFACTORY REIVE, MEN. NOW IT'S STRAIGHT HOME TO KILNOCKIE WITH THE SPOILS.

ONE THING, CAPTAIN, THE ONLY WAY BACK IS THROUGH CARLISLE... WON'T WE BE, AS IT WERE, **NOTICED** ?

OF COURSE WE WILL... ...THAT'S ALL PART OF MY **PLAN**.

MOO! MOO!

IT'S MARKET DAY... WE WILL ENTER THE CITY AS SIMPLE **CATTLE DROVERS**... WE'LL LEAVE BY THE NORTH GATE THE SAME WAY.

THEN, WE'D BETTER HURRY. THE GATES CLOSE AT **DUSK**, ...AND IT'S GETTING LATE !

CAPTAIN, I DON'T KNOW **HOW** TO BE A SIMPLE CATTLE DROVER !

SHUGGIE ! IF **YOU** CAN'T ACT SIMPLE.... ..NO-ONE CAN !

27a

KNOCK ! KNOCK ! !

WHO·O·O'S THERE ?

ARTHUR !

THIS SORT OF THING WOULD NORMALLY CONTINUE LIKE : 'ARTHUR' WHO ? —'ARTHUR' ANY MORE AT HOME LIKE YOU ?... OR SOMETHING IN SIMILAR VEIN ! BUT..THIS TIME IT REALLY **IS** ARTHUR.... STILL HOT ON THE TRAIL OF SHUGGIE !

TING!

THE SUN DIPS TOWARDS THE WESTERN HORIZON AS THE SIMPLE CATTLE DROVERS APPROACH THE SOUTH GATE OF THE CITY OF CARLISLE.....

PITY ABOUT THE **1000 MERKS** AND ALL THOSE **CATTLE** !

MY OWN TRUE **LOVE** !

HOW I GOT DOWN FROM THAT TREE.. I'LL **NEVER** UNDERSTAND.

... WHILE, ON THE BROW OF A HILL, AND THE THRESHOLD OF A NEW TOMORROW, THE FUGITIVE LOVERS, YOUNG LOCHINVAR AND THE FAIR ELLEN, PAUSE BEFORE RIDING INTO THE SUNSET AND OUT OF OUR TALE......

27b

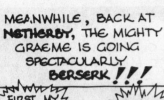

MEANWHILE, BACK AT **NETHERBY**, THE MIGHTY GRAEME IS GOING SPECTACULARLY **BERSERK** !!!

FIRST, MY DAUGHTER

NOW, MY CATTLE

THEY WON'T GET AWAY WITH IT !

I WAS **SUSPICIOUS** FROM THE START... THE BEARDED ONE IN THE **SPANISH HELMET** !

THE **EYES** GAVE HIM AWAY !

TOO CLOSE TOGETHER !

SERGEANT!

S-A-A-A-R !

PARADE THE MEN-AT-ARMS IN FIVE MINUTES, BOOTED, SPURRED AND ARMED TO THE TEETH ! ISSUE ORDER No.007(a) !

..NOT... ORDER No. **007(a)** ?

YES... 007(a) .. LICENCED TO KILL.... **SLOWLY** !

30a

I THINK WE'RE SAFE IN THIS HOLLOW.

I'M **HUNGRY** !

CAPTAIN... I'VE GOT **BLINTZES** !

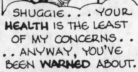

SHUGGIE... YOUR **HEALTH** IS THE LEAST OF MY CONCERNS.. ..ANYWAY, YOU'VE BEEN **WARNED** ABOUT..

NO, CAPTAIN, YOU **EAT** THEM ! THAT NICE MRS REBECCA GAVE ME THEM. THERE'S ENOUGH FOR TWO EACH.

HI, CAPTAIN, I THINK SOMEONE'S COMING

TOWN GUARD

HUE & CRY

GRAEME OF NETHERBY

30b

M-M-M! THEY'RE **114** TO OUR **5**... WE'VE GOT THE **EDGE** ON THEM..**BUT**....

..IF WE CAN SLIP AROUND THEIR REAR IN THE DARK WE MIGHT BE ABLE TO RETRIEVE THE CATTLE..

..AND BE WELL ON OUR WAY BEFORE THEY MISS EITHER THEM OR US!

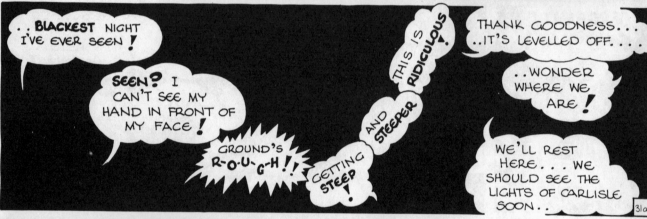

..**BLACKEST** NIGHT I'VE EVER SEEN!

SEEN? I CAN'T SEE MY HAND IN FRONT OF MY FACE!

GROUND'S **R-O-U-G-H**!!

GETTING STEEP !

AND STEEPER

THIS IS **RIDICULOUS** ▶

THANK GOODNESS... ..IT'S LEVELLED OFF....

..WONDER WHERE WE ARE!

WE'LL REST HERE... WE SHOULD SEE THE LIGHTS OF CARLISLE SOON..

31a

IT'S **COLD**... WHAT ABOUT LIGHTING A **FIRE**?

SHUGGIE... SEE IF YOU CAN FIND SOMETHING THAT MIGHT BURN!

CRUNCH!

RUSTLE!

CRACKLE!

SNAP!

CREAK!

CAPTAIN! YOU'RE NEVER GOING TO **BELIEVE** THIS..... BUT THERE'S A HUGE PILE OF **FIREWOOD** LYING OVER HERE!

YOU'RE RIGHT.. ..I **DON'T**.... STRIKE A LIGHT AND LET'S **SEE**!

RIGHT, CAPTAIN!

SCRATCH

SPARK

FLICKER!

SEE!

OOPS! I'VE BURNT MY FINGERS !

WELL! YOU WANTED A FIRE!

31b

WE'VE BEEN **TRICKED**! OLD FAWKES SAID NOTHING ABOUT CROSSING THE **SOLWAY**!

BUT.. YOU DIDN'T **ASK**.. **YOU** SAID: WHERE DOES **SCOTLAND** LIE? .. AND HE SAID: **NORTH** ... AND **THERE** IT **IS**!

PERHAPS THERE'S A **BRIDGE**!

° °. o POP! °°°° oooo

QUIET, SHUGGIE!

THIS CALLS FOR A **COUNCIL OF WAR**!

SHUGGIE! KEEP WATCH!

DO YOU THINK WE COULD..?

PERHAPS WE MIGHT...?

COULD WE?

ON THE OTHER HAND..?

..OR..

CAPTAIN... I CAN HEAR VOICES AND HORSES' HOOVES.

HUE! CLIP-CLOP!

37a

QUICK! OUT OF SIGHT!

TOO **LATE**.. ..THEY'VE SPOTTED US!

UGLY LOOKING BUNCH .. BOLDNESS IS THE BEST BET..!

GOOD DAY, GENTLEMEN!

AH, **BON JOUR**, MESSIEURS!

HUH, **FOREIGNERS**!.. NOT ONLY LOOK ALIKE.. THEY CAN'T EVEN TALK PROPER

ME.. **BLACK DICK**... LAIRD OF KILNOCKIE!

QUEL SOULAGEMENT, **MILORD DEEK NOIR**.. WE FEARED YOU ARE **LES BRIGANDS**!

I AND MY COMPAGNONS.. WE ARE HUMBLE - ER - **MERCHANTS**.. PURVEYORS OF LES OIGNONS....

YOU KEEP A **SHOP**?

NON, NON,.. WHOLESALE ONLY.. WE RETURN NOW TO OUR SHIP.

DID YOU SAY **SHIP**?

37b

NOTE FOR THOSE WHO THINK THAT **POSSES** WERE INVENTED IN THE **WILD WEST**.... FROM LEGAL LATIN: "**POSSE COMITATUS**" ... THE **POSSE** WAS ANOTHER ANCIENT SYSTEM FOR HUNTING DOWN MALEFACTORS ... MORE FORMAL THAN 'HUE AND CRY'.. ... JOINING A **POSSE** WAS STRICTLY BY **INVITATION**.

39a

MEANWHILE: BACK HOME IN **KILNOCKIE**.

FOUR DAYS THEY'VE BEEN GONE!

I ONLY WANTED SOME **BEEF**.. NOT THE **CROWN JEWELS**!

TAMMAS!..NO WORD YET OF HIS MISERABLE LORDSHIP?

NO, M'LADY, NOT A THING.

IF HE HAS ANY SENSE HE'LL STAY AWAY!

RIGHT...SADDLE MY HORSE..WE'RE GOING TO PAY A CALL ON SOMEONE WHO MIGHT **JUST** KNOW WHAT'S GOING ON!

AWKWARD OLD BESOM..**AND**..THIS MY DAY OFF

DON'T DAWDLE!

IF YOU WERE **HALF** A SERVANT YOU'D KNOW WHAT YOUR MASTER WAS **UP** TO!

WE TURN RIGHT... THEN TAKE THE FIRST LEFT...

IF I WAS HALF A MAN I'D CATCH UP AND.. I-I-I'D BITE HER.. IF I HAD ANY TEETH!

OPEN UP! THE LADY GRIZEL OF KILNOCKIE DEMANDS AUDIENCE OF **THOMAS THE RHYMER**.

40a

GOOD MORROW, YOUR LADYSHIP, WHAT DO YOU SEEK? ARE YOU ANXIOUS TO LEARN THE BEST DAY OF THE WEEK TO HANG OUT YOUR WASHING? PERHAPS I SHOULD SING OF FASHIONS FROM PARIS YOU'LL SEE IN THE SPRING? OR MAYBE...

QUIET!.. JUST TELL ME WHERE MY **LORD AND** (HA-HA!) **MASTER** HAS GOT TO.... HE'S SUPPOSED TO BE **REIVING CATTLE**.. .. NOT STRAVAIGING ABOUT THE KINGDOM!

MY TALENTS, SWEET LADY, ARE LIMITED, I CANNOT SAY WHAT IS HAPPENING **NOW**..THO' I TRY! TO PAST AND TO PRESENT MY SECOND SIGHT'S BLIND... BUT **WHAT IS TO HAPPEN** SPRINGS CLEAR TO MY MIND!

WELL... TELL ME! **TELL ME!**

-**ULP!**.. I SEEM TO HEAR FAINTLY THE SOUND OF A **BELL**..... AND THE LOWING OF MANY-SCORE **CATTLE** AS WELL. THEY ARE LED BY A **LAD** THROUGH THE STREETS OF THE TOWN..... WHILE A STRANGE-FASHIONED **OBJECT** MOVES UP AND MOVES DOWN.....

MESSAGE ENDS!

40b

41a

ON A REMOTE PART OF THE GALLOWAY COAST AN EARNEST **DISCUSSION** IS IN PROGRESS.

41b

THE URGENT DISCUSSION CONTINUES

WE **COULD** SAY THE **CATTLE** ALL FELL DOWN A **HOLE**....

.. **OR** WERE EATEN BY A **WOLF** !

WHY DON'T WE **SNEAK** IN BEFORE DAWN..

.. AND **PRETEND** THAT WE'VE NEVER BEEN **AWAY** !

LOOK ! A **MAGPIE** !

JUST **ONE** ? .. WE'RE GOING TO HAVE **BAD LUCK** !

WHAT DO YOU MEAN ... **GOING** TO HAVE !

AT LEAST WE'LL BE HOME FOR BREAKFAST.

IT'S A LONG TIME SINCE DINNER ON THE SHIP.

DO YOU THINK THE KILNOCKIE DELICATESSEN SELLS FROG LEGS AND MATZOH BALLS ?

I DON'T KNOW .. BUT THERE'S SOMEONE SELLING **PIES**.

RUN DOWN AND GET US SOME, SHUGGIE !

PIES

BUY A PIE WHERE YOU SEE THIS SIGN

HI ! MR **PIEMAN**

THIS CRAW HAS JUST FELL AFF THE WA'

43a

I'D LIKE SOME **PIES**, PLEASE !

CERTAINLY, SIR.. .. HOW MANY ?

OH ! THERE'S ME AND MARTIN AND WALTER AND THE CAPTAIN AND WINGY AND THAT MAKES .. EH .. MM ! ... .. 3 INTO 2 I CANNOT .... .. BORROW ONE .. AND. .. EH .. GIVE ME FIVE !

HERE YOU ARE .. HOPE YOU DON'T MIND MY ASKING .... YOUR NAME ISN'T '**SIMON**' BY ANY CHANCE ?

NO ?

I JUST **WONDERED**

WE CAN SPEND THE NIGHT IN THE RUINS OF CROWDIEKNOWE..

... BUT ... CROWDIEKNOWE IS ... **HAUNTED** !

DON'T TELL ME YOU BELIEVE IN **GHOSTS** !

HELP

SHRIEK ! **PEOPLE** ! .. AND YOU SAID THERE WERE **NO SUCH** THINGS !

43b

44a

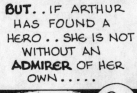

44b